I0518770

Unreliable Narrator

Poems

By

Mike Falconer

Also by Mike Falconer
Poems of Violence & Lies: A Collection
Poems of Violence & Lies: A Collection (Expanded Edition)
Working Dog: Poetry and Prose
Working Dog: Poetry and Prose (Expanded Edition)

Unreliable Narrator - Poems (1st edition — 4/12/25)
Copyright © 2025 by Mike Falconer
Doubleplusgood Media LLC.
doubleplusgoodmedia.com
ISBN: 9798992685411
ALL RIGHTS RESERVED

This book contains no AI content.
The author does not give permission for this work to be used in the training of AI models.
You are killing the arts — stop it.

These poems and this collection are fully protected under the copyright laws of The United States of America. No part of this collection may be reproduced in any manner whatsoever without the prior written permission of the author, expect or brief quotations for critical articles and reviews.

Cover design created with images provided by Mike Falconer

Chapter Quotes: Riggan, William (1981). Pícaros, Madmen, Naïfs, and Clowns: The Unreliable First-person Narrator. Univ. of Oklahoma Press: Norman.

Avantpop Publishing
Las Vegas, Nevada
avantpopbooks.com

For Cathy, Alisha, Lucinda, & Patrick

Table of Contents

Introduction

Here you shall find the latest poetic insight from writer Mike Falconer. His third collection of poetry, Unreliable Narrator, is a journey in four parts. The first two sections escort the reader through cities of social commentary, driving you past billboards of sarcasm and hypocrisy, and road-sign directions of literary discernment. As you break through the illusion that has been forming a thick wall around our society for decades, you cross over the bridge into sections three and four. Here we enter Falconer's personal neighborhood, where the streets are paved in emotion and self reflection. Once you arrive, Falconer invites you into his home, where you feel so comfortable, you begin to believe this residence could be yours.

The Unreliable Narrator is anything but unreliable. This is a book of allegories and individual tales that will have you discovering not only who Mike Falconer is but likewise who you might be as well.

Shwa Laytart

Acknowledgements

Where to start...

Let's start at the cover. A huge thank you to Sugar Laytart for creating the cover art from a semi drunken conversation during a poetry open mic in a very loud bar. It looks amazing. Many thanks to the many photographers whose pictures were hacked apart to make me look cool, particularly Robin Tucker, Lucinda Flint, and the forgotten photographer from my first appearance at Doomed Poetry.

The back cover photograph of me was taken by Arron Smith at a poetry open mic in Aberdeen Scotland, my birthplace. The photograph was taken in front of His Majesty's Theatre where I had my first job, a beautiful full circle moment.

Shwa Laytart wrote a fabulous introduction and has been one of my biggest supporters in my poetry journey. Even if Avantpop had not published this collection, Shwa would have been my first choice for the introduction. I also must separately thank Sugar and Shwa for everything that they do for the arts in Las Vegas, but most especially for their hard work in publishing this collection and making it significantly better than it would have been otherwise. You guys are the best.

Finally, I'd like to thank all the poets and the poetry fans who welcomed me with open arms, applause, advice, and friendship when I started reading in public. Writing can be a lonely passion, and you all made it worth coming out in an evening to read and to listen. I don't know what I would have done without you all and it has been my privilege to be part of your community.

For anyone I missed — I owe you a beer.

Author's Note

This book has been a long time coming. It has been split into four sections as per William Riggan's 1981 study of unreliable narrators in literature. It seemed appropriate for this collection, although I'm sure not strictly accurate. Call it artistic license, that dreaded "get out of jail free card" which gives permission for things that amuse only the author.

In early 2023, not long after I published my second book, Working Dog, I started to perform my poetry in public in my adopted hometown of Las Vegas (– Yes, Las Vegas has a poetry scene). While not the instant success that all writers dream of, what I did find was a community that was welcoming and accepting. Not only did I learn from this community, I made some great friends, and met some incredibly gifted poets and performers. To say that this community influenced my poetry would be an understatement.

Like in the expanded editions of my previous books, this volume contains QR codes which link to videos of yours truly reading each poem. If you wish to read, please read. If you want to listen, please listen. If you want to do both, have at it.

I hope you enjoy the poems.

Mike Falconer
June 2025

The Picaro

"An antihero serving as "an embodiment of the obstinacy of sin", whose "behavior is marked by rebelliousness", resentment, and aggression, and whose "world view is characterized by resignation and pessimism""

1983

Despite all the warnings
From history, literature, film, and song
We invited them in
With cute names to overcome reservations
For convenience and with the promise of saving a few dollars
Because we were scared and no longer wanted to read
Smug in our self-satisfaction that we were not North Korea,
China, or Russia without actually looking in the mirror

The billionaires are listening
Ready for fulfill our need for consumption without our having to
move from the couch

The NSA are tracking
mapping movements and behavior ready with facial recognition
and social engineering

The police are militarized
An occupying force in all but name
"Protect and Serve" propaganda and upheld as such by the
Supreme Court

We spout the phrase Orwellian without recognizing our
continuing slide on the slope it describes
Don't be betrayed by thoughts of Ingsoc and Goldstein
The flag and the Middle East work just as well for the Middle
West
This is not a science fiction yarn to put in a basket with Avatar
and Star Wars

We turned Big Brother into a fucking game show

The Department of Homeland Security
The war on Terror

Fake News
Alternative facts
The Ministry of Peace
Thought crime
New Speak
How much Doublethink does is take to accept the rebranding of
the Mujhadine (our friends) as the Taliban (our enemy)
And the Taliban (our enemy) as the new Taliban (our friend)

We are at war with Drugs, we have always been at war with drugs
We are at war with Eurasia, we have always been at war with
Eurasia

Orwell's thesis was that that control is dependent on complicity
and self-deception rather than force
That control is a goal itself

How many rights do we have to give up in the name of freedom?
Freedom is slavery

How many wars do we have to fight to defend peace?
War is Peace

The rewriting of the past by forgery at the Ministry of Truth has
given way to a lack of care for facts and history
The demonization of libraries
The banning of books
There is nothing to rewrite if we don't care to look
Even Big Brother recognized the value in forbidden poetry

We do not live in 1984
but we must recognize that it's 1983.

Machine Food

A better, brighter, future
The next big thing
A solution to all the world's problems
In plastic, software, and analytic manipulation

We are machine food
An oligarchy of bright and shiny things
Grist for the mill
A wave of the future
From the hollowed-out dreams of the past

Feeding lies of freedom and enrichment
While stealing food from the mouths of babes
Chewing on the bodies of the dispossessed
And swallowing the corpses of the undeserving

A fortune cookie at the end of the world
"An unexpected path to wealth is just ahead" reads the message
And a fucking QR code to an online poker site is on the other
side
Selling souls to cover the price of a fortune cookie

We are machine food
"Soylent Green is people."

The Greater Fool

A life as a lie
Dedicated to self-aggrandizing falsehood
Ideas withered and dying on vines of wrath
Like the shelter of a decaying tin roof

A choice
To throw it all away in a fit of despair
Or to continue on
Parading a shell of self-parody

There is no meridian where here there lies dragons
Of course, I'm the asshole
The greater fool
Overvaluing things that others consider worthless
Tilting at windmills

Being eviscerated by those one wants to be most valued by
That Don Quixote moment
The incompatibility of the practical and the aesthetic

But if that is fate
Then manifest away
The greater fool I'll be
And proud of it.

Try that in a Big City

People will be murdered by police because of the color of their skin
People will be murdered by police because they went to wrong house
People will be murdered by police because it's Tuesday
But..
Try that in a big city
There will be consequences
Not enough
And certainly not justice
But there will be video
There will be outrage
There will be protests
There will be awareness that a crime has taken place

People will be pushed into despair, drug abuse, and homelessness
A system that can't do the math of prevention vs. punishment
People will be forgotten because society does not seem to care
But try that in a big city
There will be services
There will be those who care
While options are rarely perfect
And there is a long way to go
Mental health problems are recognized as just that – mental health problems
The criminalization of existence edges back from the abyss

Trans kids die because of bullying, a lack of acceptance, and not being able to be the person they are
The denial of care in the name of protecting children by people who could not care less about children
Try that in a big city
Gender affirming care has a better long term success rate than knee surgery or hip replacement

Pronouns, rainbows, and understanding are the norm for the urban and suburban

A woman's right to choose is under attack
A rolling back of civil rights unthinkable a few short years ago
Children forced to leave their state because religion is more important than their life
But try that in a big city
Abortion is matter between a woman and her doctor
Not her doctor, their lawyer, their congressman — it's always a man — and their preacher

A country music singer runs from the stage during a mass shooting
Taking his microphone and platform without warnings or help for those left in the line of fire
Try that in a big city
And there will be understanding and a lack of judgement
Because they were the victim of a crime
An atrocity
And the macho bullshit spouted on courthouse steps and music videos is not the same as a response to fear

Fuck your small town.

.

Wildfire

And I woke up to the end of the world
Apocalypse of movies and fantasy
Ash falling from the sky like leaves
The sun a blood orange
Smoke filling the air
Noxious and acrid
Blown in on Californian tides
As the west burns

Polluting the artificial as nature intended
Mountains vanished overnight
The horizon transported to the Midwest plains
Tall buildings, neon and video glamour, flattened to earth tones
Like a sepia photograph
Lost at the bottom of a drawer

But this is just an inconvenience
The fall out of forestry mismanagement and climate change
Not real the fallout of Threads or of The Day After
Horrors delivered by television
When the populace could be scared

Because it is the acceptance that is heartbreaking
That the earth hemorrhages smoke that blankets two states
And the interruption of daily runs and pool time are what seem
to matter
Where is the outrage, the tears for trees
A public resource managed for private profit

Perhaps I will go back to bed.
It is the end of the world after all.

The Point of Dystopia

The Greek word Utopia was brought into common English usage
By Sir Thomas Moore
His 16th century book of the same name
Described an idyllic island of equality
A society run for the benefit of is citizens
Utopia means literally "no place."
From there it was a hop, skip, and a jump
To the word dystopia

How do we know when we are living in a utopia vs. a dystopia?

Can we agree that a minimum quality of any society
Never mind a utopia
Has to be that it is run for the benefit of its inhabitants?

Anyone feel like they live in a society that is run for their
benefit?

If our society is not for its people
Then what is it for?

What is the point?

Joseph Schumpeter was an early 20th century political
economist
He is responsible for the concept of the entrepreneur
He also popularized the concept of "creative destruction"
That new ideas would lead to the destruction of the old ways of
doing things
and that it was the driver of growth in an economy
That capitalism was an evolutionary process
However, he also believed the capitalism would eventually
collapse

Weakened by the very things that pushed it forward
Ending in corporatism run by elites

How do we know when we are living in a utopia vs. a dystopia?

If something is bad for people working in an economy
But good for the economy

What is the point?

Who is the economy for?

In the middle of the 20th century, mathematician and,
considered by many, the inventor of the modern computer, Alan
Turing, proposed the imitation game
More commonly known as the Turing test
The imitation game was a test for a machine
to fool a human
into thinking that the machine
was human

We are in the midst of the great AI revolution
With its promise of freedom from drudgery,
and a new generation of tools and productivity

However, art was first

Art the refuge
Art the joy bringer
Art the context giver

Whose drudgery and productivity is this AI revolution for the
benefit of?

How do we know when we are living in a utopia vs. a dystopia?

Technological improvements that don't bring improvements
but just destruction of the things that we most value

What is the point?

There is a surprising lack of reverse Turing tests in this AI
revolution
A test to separate what is machine regurgitated rather than
human created
The lack of footnotes with generative AI
would seem to be useful addition for a "tool"
Stimmed by over protection of algorithmic secrets
Or perhaps potential evidence in copyright infringement lawsuits
And then there is the insistence on the marketing friendly term
"A.I"
Rather than the more accurate machine learning

Machine learning is what humans have previously created
Scraped from the internet
Stuffed into a blender
And output to decent summarization engines
and lukewarm guessing machines
without a thought to copyright and intellectual property

We will sleepwalk into AI invading the workplace
Learning from us
Getting better because of us
Replacing us because it is cheaper
But eventually failing because of a lack of new data

We are the Ouroboros
The snake eating its own tale
From the ancient Egyptian "Enigmatic Book of the Netherworld"
From the tomb of Tutankhamun
A funeral text of prescience
From a people long gone

How do we know when we are living in a utopia vs. a dystopia?

Sam Altman, is the CEO of OpenAI,
originally a non-profit focused on AI safety
But now a for profit company, that is most widely known for
ChatGPT,
And the internal infighting over the lies and riches of temptation
Altman has said multiple times onstage and in his own blog
"AI will most likely lead to the end of the world, but in the
meantime, there will be great companies created with serious
machine learning."
When Michael Crichton wrote "your scientists were so
preoccupied with whether or not they could, they didn't stop to
think if they should."
He was talking about bringing dinosaurs back from the dead, not
making poor people poorer and rich people richer.

Tech Bros can't even make a printer that works

What is the point?

The Artificial Intelligence apocalypse
Will not be killer robots who look like Arnold
(a lot less of those kinds of movies of late for those not paying
attention)
The Infopocalypse will be algorithmically incoherent
An internet of machines talking to machines
Manipulating and obfuscating to the highest bidder
"Alexa, "should I leave my wife"
Answered by averages and random chance
The opinion of machines more important than the opinions
people
The death of the internet as a tool is probably already here
With Reddit the default result on Google for almost everything
Since when did Reddit become the arbiter of truth?

How do we know when we are living in a utopia vs. a dystopia?

According to Greek myth
When Pandora opened a box in the care of her husband
All the evils of the world were released
Slamming it shut too late she trapped hope in the box

We live in a world of technologies that are artificially limited
Or forced into failure
For the benefit of "society" rather than the people in that society
Copyright only seems to matter to those who can punch
downwards
Your iPhone can't have a headphone jack
So we can sell you Bluetooth headphones for hundreds of dollars
Our books, movies, and music are not owned
But at the whims of a subscription model and changing licensing
agreements
Cloud based document sharing to put paid to paper
And those pesky printers
Selling ink that costs more than the printer was just not quite
good enough

The promise of lies
The lies of promise

What is the point?

If we can limit and implement technology for benefit of
corporations, billionaires, and the status quo it can be limited and
implemented for people

Are we in a pot of slowly boiling water?

The fable goes, that a frog will jump out if placed in a pot of
boiling water
But will be slowly cooked alive if placed in cool water that is
incrementally heated
However, what actually happens if you place a frog into boiling
water, is that it dies

And if you place a frog into cool water, it jumps out because it
can

Can we jump out of the pot, or have we already been dumped
into the boiling water?
Not using AI will require the courage of our convictions
That being creative does not always have to be destructive
That moving fast and breaking things just leads to broken things
That societies should be for the benefit of all the people inside
them
And that we all get to decide what the point is

Do we live in a utopia or a dystopia?

And So Things Changed...

It started with three shots to the back

Deny
Defend
Depose

The killing of a multi-millionaire CEO
Rich on the back of claim denial
How appropriate for American change
to come from the barrel of a gun
Rather than the killing of classrooms of children

The 1% of the 1% begged for forgiveness
A realization that their oligarchy came from exploitation
That the game was rigged in their favor
And so we should all just stop playing
The misery of the majority
Fed on dreams of avarice
While choking on propaganda and lies
Of the American nightmare they dreamt of

So in fear of a tale of two cities
Health care became universal
The homeless housed through basic income
Politics meant service rather than riches
The soldiers laid down their weapons
No longer the servants of hegemony
The police upheld the law rather than enforced it
A right to not get shot
Rather than a right to shoot
Renewables given the subsidies of the polluters
Food became free of pesticides and price gouging
Public transportation replaced road building

Power accountable to the powerless

A country for the people and of the people
Became more than words of control
The billionaires became millionaires
Paying their fair share of taxes
For the benefit of all

A bloodless revolution in how we all chose to live
Started through the spilling of blood

One can dream.

 # A Poem for while you are Pooping

So here we are
We two
You picking up a poetry book
And me writing about you pooping
We both have some shit to get rid of

Feel superior while you work out your posterior
Your friends and family are all on their smart phones
Watching TikToks and pretending to not scroll through Facebook
Hopefully nobody is gathering content for Instagram

Revel in this alone time
We get so little in our self-imposed media saturation
That is of course if the dog leaves you alone
And the cat stops watching

This is the room without a television
Except the one masquerading as a telephone
Exceptions of course for the Uber rich
Maybe that will be the line in the sand
The first against the wall when the revolution comes
"TV in your bathroom?"
Against the wall you go

Although the inverse, a book of poetry, might be an equidistant
line
Sorry dear reader
If that's the case take heart
for I'll have already been against that wall

How are things moving along?
Has all this talk of revolution and media helped or hindered?
It is of course the reality of our world for terms to be
appropriated and neutered

Revolution should mean blood in the streets
Not the new iPhone

So if all this sphincter puckering has not ruined your alone time
Let me leave you with one final thought before the toilet paper
and flush

To question the status quo, the comforts and convenience, that
imprison us
Has gotten a bad wrap
The Luddite's, forever misunderstood, 19th century grassroots
movements suck at marketing, had a point

If you are reading these scatalogical prose on the porcelain
throne
You are already fighting against that steady and constant pull
The suck of dopamine addiction
And the quest for internet fame

So I salute you pooper for fighting back against the tide
One poem, one dump, at a time.

The Clown

"A narrator in the tradition of the fool, the court jester and the sotie, whose unreliable narration includes "irony, variations of meaning, ambiguities of definition, and possibilities for reversal and counter-reversal""

A Home for Goldilocks

Goldilocks was walking through the forest one day,
When she came across a dilapidated house.
She had been persecuted all her life because of her golden hair,
and a proper home of her own sounded great.
"This used to be the home of my ancestors" she thought to herself.
And so, she went right in.

The house was obviously a home.
With three beds upstairs and food in the pantry.
There were even three bowls of porridge cooling on the kitchen table.
"This has always been my house really,"
Goldilocks continued to think to herself.
"Sure, it's changed hands quite a bit,
But it's still my home."

Soon three bears came to the house.
"This is our home," said the Bears.
Goldilocks readily agreed, but asked if she could stay.
The bears agreed that she could sleep on the floor.
And they remained silent on the subject of Goldilocks having eaten Mama Bear's porridge.

But soon Goldilocks was not happy with just sleeping on the floor.
She slipped into Baby Bear's bed, even though it was too small for her, and pushed him out.
"Who's sleeping in my bed?" wailed Baby Bear
Daddy Bear became angry and shouted at Goldilocks.
But Goldilocks refused to be cowed and shouted back claiming the bed as her own.

A passing woodsman heard the ruckus.

"That house would make a perfect strategic outpost in this conflict region," thought the Woodsman.

He entered the house and told the Bears and Goldilocks to be quiet.

That they would have to share the house.

The Woodsman did not have much time for Bears, "troublemakers" he thought.

At the same time, he recognized Goldilocks as the daughter of the widow he wanted to play hide the salami with.

And so, he wanted Goldilocks out of the way.

This house, and this set of circumstances, seemed perfect.

The Woodsman wrote an agreement for sharing the house.

The agreement said that it was the Bears home.

But it also said that Goldilocks had the right to the house as her home.

Both the Bears and Goldilocks signed the agreement feeling they had each got what they wanted.

But they continued to argue, as the agreement was fundamentally flawed.

Because Baby Bear's bed was too small for Goldilocks,

She wanted to rest her feet on Mama Bear's bed.

"Who's been sleeping in my bed" cried Mama Bear.

This kind of thing continued for weeks.

Finally, the Woodsman, having had enough, just left.

Leaving Goldilocks and the Bears alone to sort it out.

Goldilocks sent messages to all her relations.

Saying that they were welcome to join her in "her" home.

"Wait a minute" said Daddy Bear as Goldilocks' brothers and sisters arrived and started to climb into bed with the Bears.

But soon Daddy bear was pushed into the Attic and Mama Bear and Baby Bear were pushed into the Cellar.

The bathroom, kitchen, bedroom, living room and front door all fell under the control of Goldilocks and her family.

But Goldilocks was scared.
The Bears were big and powerful, and the forest was full of other bears who might want to intervene for six days.
So, Goldilocks sent word to her mother, who now was getting regularly boned by the Woodsman, asking for weapons and material support.

And the Woodsman delivered.
Not only because he was making good money selling arms,
And because of this new strategic ally in the region,
But because he was also in bed with Goldilocks' mother.
A lot.

Every time Mama Bear wanted to go out into the forest for food,
She had to pass through checkpoints set up by Goldilocks and be searched.
Baby Bear was allowed to work in the house for Goldilocks, making the beds that had once belonged to his family.
Daddy Bear was often refused permission to leave the attic, as he was a security threat.

After months of isolation, one day Daddy Bear snapped.
He tore off Goldilocks' brother's head and threw it across the room after being turned back at a checkpoint.
He had just wanted to see Mama Bear and Baby Bear.

Daddy Bear's paws were zipped tied behind his back and he was executed by Goldilocks' Defense Force.
His body was dumped into an unmarked mass grave.
The Cellar was attacked continually by Goldilocks.
She demanded that the remaining Bears surrender the terrorists they were hiding.
Mama Bear and Baby Bear swore that it was just them in the Cellar,

But the attacks continued.

Soon Goldilocks and her family entered the Cellar and dragged-out Mama Bear by her hair.
People from the village had heard what was happening in the house and cried out "please stop this – free the bears!"
The other bears in the forest added their voices – "Free the Bears."
But the Woodsman and Goldilocks' Mother were also there.
"Goldilocks has a right to defend herself" they said.
So, Goldilocks put a 9mm semi- automatic pistol to Mama Bear's head and blew her brains out in front of her mother, the woodsman, the people of the village, bears of the forest, and Baby Bear who cried and cried for his land, Daddy Bear, and Mama Bear.

Everyone went home.
Goldilocks and her brothers and sisters returned to their fortress.
Warily eyeing the bears from the forest.
The people of the village returned to their homes.
They were too scared of Goldilocks.
Of what she might do, and of being accused of not liking people with gold hair.
However, behind their backs, the people of the village whispered that Goldilocks had lost her soul and any sense of morality.
But did not feel strongly enough to intervene.

The Woodsman and Goldilocks' mother went home to wash their hands, get laid, and forget their worries now that the problem of the bears in the house had been solved by someone other than themselves.

And Baby bear was left out in the cold to die.
Because he no longer had a state,
or any land,
or a home,
or a family.

Aliens Bearing Gifts

Independence day was the day the earth stood still
Their flying saucers hovering over the most recognizable of major cities
The ones with landmarks that look good on TV
With their death rays and plans for invasion
Prepared to steal our water, snatch our bodies, and protect ourselves from ourselves
Mars attacks and the war of the worlds
It was the day that a UFO landed on the White House lawn
Because it's traditional
Little green men walking down a ramp saying "take me to you leader"

...and then they ran away
Flew away as fast as the laws of movie physics would allow
With a new appreciation for the dark forest theorem

But it was not because of our military might
or tenacity
Or Wells' microbes
or being quiet
or a song by Slim Whitman

What ET found was a people in need of universal healthcare and the ability to go to the dentist
Whole nations in need of hope for the future and a promise of things getting better
Or just food and clean water
Consumers wanting refuge from predatory capitalism or just to not to be only considered consumers
A world being burned down around its inhabitants in the name of GDP and the disputing of climate change consensus
A life supporting environment poisoned by those who need it most

Humanity did not want to fight back, to resist
Humanity wanted to be taken away
Not just a willing alien abduction, but a demanded one
This was no longer an invasion
It was more like a rescue mission

The other world life forms wanted no part of this tragedy
Even xenomorphs have standards
And they left saying "don't flatter yourselves"
So we were to be forever alone in the universe
Because we could not get our shit together.

Crocodile Tears - A True Story

I am the ultimate predator
Unchanged since the time of the dinosaurs
We and my kin have been here beyond memory
We have seen glaciers advance and recede
Continents split and form
Fire of the gods fall from the sky
And rise from the ground

Yet it is man who plagues our world
The death and destruction he leaves in his wake
He hunts us
Like we hunt him
But while we hunt to eat
He hunts for our skins and for trophies
With his numbers and machines
His encroachment and his poisons
We can but nibble at the edges of his world

So we make our home where we can

I and my family live in place that the men call Ramree Island
In the mangrove swamps
Living as we have always lived
While men unleash their powers against each other
Fire and metal
Machine against machine
And we die because we are inconvenient
In the way of their senseless slaughter
Their cannibalistic over consumption of themselves

Of late, the noise and destruction has been close to my home
All we can do is shelter where we are
And listen to their machines

And to their self-destruction
To men dying by man

However one night
A thousand men ran into our home
To make it their own
They were tired, hungry, and scared
They sought refuge, safety and sleep

But this is our home
And while their weapons are fearsome
So are we

We feasted like never before
With the tables turned in our favor
A hunting ground of our choosing
We grabbed and rolled
Pulling them under the water
And ate all that moved

The night was filled with the sound of the screams of man
And the sound of centuries of revenge
A feast to tell of to our young
The night we fought back

Enough for everyone
A re-ascendancy to the throne of apex predator
For one long night
The men outside our swamp called us their allies
They should not
We would just have easily eaten you
And you would have deserved it just as much

In the years since
The "worst animal attack ever recorded" as man called it
Has been called into question by men who were not there
Who would tremble in our presence

But I and my kin remember
Just as we remember the birds the next day
Cleaning the meat from our teeth

This may be the world of man
But I do not cry for you
A reminder that while your technology insulates you
We will still be here when you are gone

Feeding on your bones.

Jesus Saves

Jesus saves
Jesus saves

Everything must go
20% off all sale items
Value for money and fresh for everyone

Jesus saves
Jesus saves

Self-checkout memberships
Curbside pickup
And online ordering

Jesus saves
Jesus saves

No overnight parking
Press for an associate
Buy three for the price of two

Jesus saves
Jesus saves

Baked fresh today
Membership rewards
You saved $3.26

Jesus saves
Jesus saves

We care and thank you for shopping with us
Please show your receipt
If alarm sounds wait for a member of staff

Jesus saves
Jesus saves

Instructions for food stamps
Minimum wage
Zero-hour contracts

Jesus saves
Jesus saves

We are but the instrument of oppression
Capital and shareholder value
Tax free by avoidance and acts of Congress

Jesus saves
Jesus saves

Method in our madness
Disciples in the checkout lane
Everyday low prices at Jesus Saves.

A Las Vegas Fog

Vegas is a movie
With George Clooney and Brad Pit standing sharp suited at the bar
While Bradley Cooper and the gang of not quite so famous nurse a hangover
And Hunter S. Thompson fears and loathes all that can be indulged and exploited
A Rat Pack of dreams
"Vegas is not ready for us" says the tourist upon whom this edifice of ziggurats was built

Vegas is a mirror
A gaudy assault on the senses
The sins and miracles of Midwesterners and coastal elites
Laid bare, a reflection of America underneath the mask of church and flag
The mocking of stone throwers returning to their glass houses, riverboat casinos, and online sportsbooks
"Viva Las Vegas" the man said, holding chips and a free cocktail that cost him his mortgage payment

Vegas is a ladder
Those reaching for the stars
Or those pretending to be a few rungs higher than they are
Or pretending to slum it with indulgences and fantasies of self-destruction
Others sliding to the bottom for real, their return ticket sold for an extra spin
"You are not ready for Vegas" say the locals

Vegas is a culture
The poets and musicians gathering in bars and bookshops
While the artists paint the walls of buildings within the city limits
Their truth more alive through juxtaposition

An awareness of how the world sees and how the world is
With theatre and song as a gateway drug
"You don't know us" says the writer, poolside on a summer's day

Vegas is an underground
A network of tunnels and homelessness
The victims of gentrification, hostile architecture, and the
illegality of being unsightly on the streets
A refuge from the sun
Fatally ripped away with every monsoon season
"You don't belong here" say the Mole People with good reason

There is a mist over Vegas
A Las Vegas fog of perception and myth
Who needs the mob when you have shareholders and venture
capitalists
When what is needed is public transportation if we can't have
free parking
A destination and a home
"You live in Vegas?" Asks the ones who have never been and sit
in judgement.

Weapons

I am the lone booker

The mass reading event
To riddle the bodies of people with fresh ideas
The reading lust a decimation of ignorance

Feared by all who measure intellectual stimulation in hours
watched
Hysteria of words on a page
Written in blood, sweat, & tears
An epidemic of literate violence

Fear in the eyes of the shopped and dropped
The loner narrative dictated by those who's connections are
through the one-way mirror of a screen

And so to read a book

To scare the gatekeepers of morality with the weapons of truth,
hope, beauty, and dreams
If I am to be feared let it be for my words
For words can change things
Words can affect and have an effect

Show me a gun that can do that.

Three Men in a Bar

Batman, Luke Skywalker, and James Bond are sitting in a bar discussing terrorism

""The Oxford dictionary definition of terrorism is;

"the unlawful use of violence and intimidation, especially against civilians, in the pursuit of political aims."

That makes you both terrorists."

says James Bond

"Why "unlawful"?
Are violence and intimidation ever lawful?
Planting bombs in people's devices and blowing them up by remote control is not terrorism?
But planting bombs on yourself and blowing up yourself and other people is terrorism?"

questions Luke Skywalker

"If the state does those things, it is lawful.
A license to kill, don't you know."

responds 007 sipping his martini

"But what about Justice – right and wrong.
Invading a country, destroying its infrastructure, and murdering its people is not terrorism according to you.
But planting an improvised bomb by the roadside to blow up the vehicles of the invaders of your land is terrorism?
One can be right, yet still be unlawful."

says Batman

"So,"

says a confused Luke Skywalker.

"Dropping bombs on poor people from airplanes or directing missiles through a home's window from warships is not terrorism; however, taking over an airplane and flying it into a building is terrorism?"

"I think you are on shaky ground there kid,"

says the Dark Knight finishing his 3rd glass of Prosecco and raising it in the air for another

"Freedom fighters are not terrorists"

says Mr. Bond

"But I'm a freedom fighter – a leader of a rebellion against an unjust empire"

ventures Luke

"you are part of the rebel alliance and a traitor..."

says Bond with a smirk

"If you are part of a uniformed military unit then perhaps you would not be a terrorist"

he continues

"So if I have money backing my actions I'm ok even my actions could be considered wrong?"

says the farm boy from Tatooine, drinking and leaving himself with a blue milk mustache

"Yes of course, I like beating up poor people who are wrong and instilling in them a sense of fear. Who doesn't!"

Growls Batman

"Running around inside the Death Star shooting at Stormtroopers is terrorism.
But blowing up the Death Star, using a squadron of X-wing fighters, killing everyone inside is not"

responds Bond

"That makes no sense,"

says the destroyer of the Death Star

"Welcome to the Justice system"

says Batman

"Next you'll be saying that placing landmines all over the countryside so that they kill and maim farmers for years after a conflict that has otherwise left their land is not terrorism"

states Luke

"It's not" says James fiddling with the olive in his martini.

"You kill people for a living, I have a code"

Batman says

"And who elected you?"

Retorts Bond

"Just because you are a billionaire does not make the world your playground to do with as you wish.

The laws still apply to you.
If you want to make a difference, get involved — not hide out in a cave.
Be a good example for your peers and those that look up to you.
Work for the people and the society you are so determined needs change but only on your own terms."

From the other side of the bar comes a voice;

"The solution to terrorism is to stop committing it."

Noam Chomsky continues

"Or at least admit that terrorism is what we call it when it is done to us. Just not when we do it to others."

"SHUT UP"

says Batman, Luke Skywalker, and James Bond in unison

The three men's only point of agreement of the evening as they continue drinking themselves into oblivion without resolution.

The Madman

"A narrator who is untrustworthy due to an "unbalanced mind" whose narration serves as a case study in the pathology of insanity."

Simple Obsessions

Whispers from another stranger's road
Scratchings in the margins of a Gideon bible
Passages imprinted on the last pages of a hotel note pad
A scribbled addition to the room service menu

A simple obsession
Communicating with unseen past travelers
In the secret places we share
The people who we would never meet
Meeting through the detritus of leavings

Someone else's boarding pass
Used as a bookmark in a book exchanged
The fantasies in origami gifts
Hidden at the back of a drawer
A scrap of paper in the battery compartment of a TV Remote

The places that belong to a traveler
And survive the decontamination of people making minimum
wage
Gifts for the very skilled
Or extremely lucky

Human connection from those that abhor it at every other turn
The places that don't belong to locals
The stranger reading a book at the bar
There for food, alcohol, and little else

Connection without connecting
In a world that prefers home to anywhere else
What to do when home is not an option?
Not the horror of homelessness
But the despair of less than a home

So allow me this obsession
The intersection of past and present
A tap into an unseen world
The breadcrumbs of lifted vails
The secrets we hold and only tell to strangers

And maybe to ourselves
Alone in the dark
Of somewhere that's not home.

A Shadow in the Distance

The first time I saved your life
You were sitting on a couch
A razor blade in your hand
Plans interrupted by a knock at the door

It was over a girl of course
Out of options, and a future
Humiliated in your own mind
Friend zoned to within an inch of your life

The second time I saved your life
It was coming home too soon
A drink of bitter liquid death
Chased by pills, alcohol, and a knot of despair

Work and anxiety was the culprit this time
Unable to see the wood for the trees
The story for the story in one's head
The end of a way of life to protect a life

The third time I saved your life
It was a noose around your neck
Talking you out of upsetting the chair
Loosening ropes against changing of your mind

Surprise surprise, a girl again
Run around and no time this time around
Fear of being forever alone
A lack of compatibility with the human race

And so here we are
A future neither of us could have foreseen
Who knew that age would stymie the rage
Disappointment is now just that –

Disappointment
The alternatives almost welcome

Of course it's always a companion
A reminder of a dark path not taken
A shadow in the distance
But not today, no not today

Pain

Mum said the pain was bad this week

Scared to know how to ask for help
Mortality beginning to dawn on this 92-year-old woman who has been a constant in my life
"Bury us all" is beginning to look like tempting fate
I'm wondering how long our weekly transatlantic phone calls will continue
The "I love you sign off" that only happens when one of us is scared

That fucking programmed British reserve rearing its ugly head yet again.

So of course, I question my life choices
The decision to get as far away as possible as quickly as possible from what feels parochial and provincial
Knowing she would kick my ass for changing a thing
But I still chose to leave and stay away

The guilt is as real as the justifications

How can I not look at futures end?
The singularly after which everything changes
Death is an ugly truth somehow made mundane

I can't believe I've leveraging this moment in a poem

But isn't this my truth?
How else to deal with it?

A Gift of a Book

Poems of old
Thoughtful in return for thought provoking
Written words for the written word
An author's blacked out signature in a signed edition

A value of forty cents.
A new inscription, new meaning, and new value.

A mark of friendship
Uncomfortable as unmasked feelings are to those who should be
the least concerned
For others there is acceptance of a newfound identity
That prompts a return to exploration after a soul laid bare

What greater gift?

A Perfect Match

Thinking about you
A race to feel, feelings
The struggle with impatience and the passage of time
Hurry up and fall in love
Delete the apps
The dignity of banishment of memory.

Get it done
Start the run
The deep dive past the small talk
The intimacy of peeling back layers
Uncertainty and caution
The emotional safety of men
The physical safety of women.

The perfect match
Never so simple
Hallucinations of the future
The channeling of the love songs of lone guitars
Waiting for walls to be broken down?
The games that were not to be played.

There goes those ghosts again
Putting into shadow the dawning light
But this poem is not going to go there
Rather we'll look to the possibilities
The future noir of being our best
Social media coming outs
And the juggling act of being what we want to be

Fear of apathy and a lack of relevance
Shaky foundations looking for new pillars of reinforcement
A certain resignation is a dark cloud on a summer's day

Too much control, too much past and too much age for getting
lost
Again.
I am adrift, not looking for rescue, but how to swim.

The End of the Climb

A jarred back
Twisted knee
Not the injury of nightmares
The injury of age

What am I doing here?
Replaced by "I don't belong"
Am I doing this because I feel I should?
Rather than for enjoyment, no longer there

Tempus fugit
The end of the climb
When risk outweighs reward
When obligation increases gravity

If the why becomes self-identity
Then self-identity may need to change
Life is too short
Happy or right, rather than neither.

The Naïf

"The naïf narrator lacks the experience "to deal in any far-reaching manner with the moral, ethical, emotional, and intellectual questions which arise from his first ventures into the world and from his account of those ventures.""

Perfume and Roses

I give you perfume
and roses
Like I bring
the specter
of divorce
Kisses that make
you tremble
And words
to give you
goosebumps

We fell into
whatever
this was
These snatched moments
in elevators and museums
The scandalizing
of room service waiters
Selfies from a different life
taken just for me

I'm not excusing
my moral failings
Just like I don't care
about yours
But in my defense
You seemed miserable
and lonely
And I made you
happy

I'm not the one
that got between you

and him
You guys did that
all by yourselves
But you decided
to bring him back
between us
Wrecking
my
world
Choosing status quo
and cowardice

But bitterness
is unbecoming
Replaced by silent
sadness
Memory of connection
and reciprocating selflessness
The love story lies
of books and movies

The sin of
lovers
The freedom to
dream
While looking at
each others eyes
Through bars of
a self made
Prison

A language of
the unsaid
Results of listening
to offhand remarks
Proof of listening

to someone who
is not listened too
My gifts of
perfume and roses
Monuments
to folly and failure

Measured in
memory
Treasured by
one
exiled to
another life
by
another.

Talisman Alone

"You are here" the sign says
Unwilling to settle
Knowing the destructive place
Punishing someone for not being someone else
For I have known perfection
And I have been rejected by it

A fate accepted if not all together tolerated
A bridge long burned
It's pylons collapsed and at the bottom of the darkest of rivers
But a pain still flammable
Kept candles framed by the prison of patterns

Time like flood channels
But still trapped
I don't believe in angels
But the demons believe in me
Clinging to politeness and kindness
Like a talisman
Alone

The stream of other lives
A rock in the flow
Covered in the algae slime of envy
Madness of those on the fringes of acceptability
Sarcophagi of self immolation

You can't die in your dreams
But you can dream

The nightmares say so

Alpha Male

Who does not cry at the end of movies?
When the dog dies
Or when their father is on stage giving the speech of his life?

Comfortable enough in my own masculinity
I can admit some things
I cry at things that matter
Like poetry, music, and at the end of movies
When the dog dies

Real men are not afraid to have emotions
To share them
Just like any he/him she/her they/them

If this triggers you then perhaps alpha male is not what you think
it is

I make things, I write things,
I work with my hands, I work with my mind
I speak to those who need to hear
I speak to those who want to listen
I employ people and try to be fair, equitable, and a promoter of
integrity

And I would never be so crass as to define myself as an "alpha
male"
I don't really care what people think
I just care that they think

The software industry labels something as "alpha" when it needs
testing and will have major errors

"Beta" testing being where the errors are less pronounced

The stage before software, the instructions for making things work, is ready for the grown-up world

Empathy is not the antithesis of masculinity

It should define it

A solution to masculinity that is toxic

The intellectual

The gentleman

The well read

These are terms that the world needs to be more proud of instead of

The influencer

The billionaire

The alpha male

The dictator

Those who define themselves by the level of oppression they can inflict

And the shallowness of their ideas

The hate that runs in their veins

Alpha male is just another word for A-Hole.

Memories of Never Being

I miss that that never was
Our interactions so fluid and effortless
Compatibility meets timing
For once on the right side of circumstance

And yet not
For there are always obstacles
Hazards in the roadway
And so not to be

There is a possible yet in that last sentence
But possibilities are not promises
And promises are not facts
Tethered yet adrift

Time is but the passing of possibilities
A shortening of opportunity and hope
Lead down alleys of scam and fish
A reckoning of middle age and isolation

For the words that are never heard
A poem to overvalued interactions
There is but memories of never being
The never was that never could

As sand drops through an hourglass
Life bleeds away
And the punishments of yesteryear become aspirational
Like the memes of dying social platforms

For whom bells toll
Are but the observers and commentators

The myth makers and authors of revelation
To be ignored and dismissed

Like the memories of never being.

Old White Guy

I'm an old white guy
How the fuck did that happen?

Straight – with a few predilections just like everyone else – white,
and old

British, Scottish to be truly accurate
You might have noticed

I do not share the guilt of southern slave owner forbearers
I share the guilt of empire building classists who raped and
pillaged half the world...
And helped invent southern slave trade

Sure we help create the abolitionist movement too
but that's like saying "I no longer beat my wife"

Call me ally if you must, but it is a title I'm not sure I deserve
I am here to be uncomfortable
To recognize that I will never recognize
I can't speak, even in fiction, to the inconceivable
I'm not a person of color
I'm not gay, I'm not trans, I'm not marginalized from my position
of privilege
Even my outsider status as a holder of a piece of plastic with
green card written on it hardly makes a dent in that
They even want my vote
Although they can't have it
Pledging allegiance is just a step too far

Just being able to say these words is cloaked in a privilege I
didn't earn
But that I was born with

Born to Anglo Saxon white Protestant parents
One dead, one dying

So I'm here for truth
To hear truth
Maybe even to speak it
Exercising my privilege to be welcomed
Or even just tolerated
Without fear other than nerves
As that old white guy.

Pareidolia

Pictures of old girlfriends
I put them in a box
The relationships and my emotions about them
The photos hid in a computer folder
Indexed and catalogued
A box of ones and zeros

Just because you close a wound
Does not stop it hurting
Memories jostling to be ghosts or the moved on
But memories are scabs
Always ready to be picked over
To bleed
Never allowed time to turn into scars
And pictures just seemed like a bad idea

Do faces in those old photographs
Taken to immortalize a moment in time
Think about what was?
Do they have their own scabs to pick over
Or are there just scars
Memory of time passed and little else

But maybe it's time to let go
Time to put down the carried torches
Extinguish the flames that were once fuel

So now the pictures are in frames
Hung on walls
They are my scars
And if thoughts linger too much...
there is pain
But doesn't that validate what we once had?
Memories of the good and the bad

Running away was always cowardice
Hiding not that much better
So it is time for the pictures to see the light of day
For my acknowledgement of their part
In my story
And if it hurts
The melancholy is to be treasured
Like the faces on the wall.

A Requiem for a Bookshop

Free books
Books by the pound
Great books for $2.00
Books by local authors
Books by those who don't get into bookshops

Art and tarot
UFOs and weed
Hunter and Burroughs
Billy Bragg and H.L.T. Quan
Zines and chaps
Stickers and postcards
Signed and rare
The weird, the silenced, the banned, and the marginal

And poetry
So much poetry
Enough for a heart-full

A cultural nexus
A haven and open to all
Events, outreach, and selfless
In a town that always has to fight for artistic recognition
A town with an inexhaustible capacity to shoot itself in the foot
In a country where the National Endowment for the arts is
0.003% of the federal budget
A country that needs far more art and far less weapons

How to define a great bookshop?
By how much it will be missed.

About The Author

Originally hailing from Scotland, and after a career in the entertainment lighting business, Mike is the Hospital Administrator for a 14-doctor veterinary practice, and two satellite practices in Las Vegas.

A Hospital Administrator for 18 years, Mike also writes, speaks, and consults on management, human resources, marketing, and social media. A Top Writer on Quora, winner of the Founders Award from the Uncharted Veterinary Conference, and frequent poster to his own blog, Mike is also involved in various veterinary management, human resources, and marketing organizations.

In his spare time, Mike is a voracious reader, consumer of film, theater patron, renovates his house, watches hockey games, and dabbles in Yoga and hiking; both of which he does badly. He lives in North Las Vegas with his two dogs; a greyhound called Ella, and a mutt called Miles who is slowly destroying his house.

Mike's first volume of poetry; Poems of Violence and Lies, was published in 2022 and his second; Working Dog – Poems and Prose, was published in 2023.

Facebook: facebook.com/wordoutlet
Instagram: @word_outlet
TikTok: tiktok.com/wordoutlet
BlueSky: @wordoutlet.bsky.social
wordoutlet.net – Poetry and Prose
mikefalconer.net – Business essays and book reviews

www.ingramcontent.com/pod-product-compliance
Lightning Source LLC
Chambersburg PA
CBHW011225120626
46545CB00010B/3152